Taste of Korea

Korean Cuisine Full of
Wisdom and Nature

Taste of Korea: Korean Cuisine Full of Wisdom and Nature

Edited and Published by
Korean Spirit & Culture Promotion Project
http://www.kscpp.net

Photo by Jae-sik Suh

ISBN: 978-0-9797263-9-2

First print, April 2008

Printed in the Republic of Korea

Taste of Korea

Korean Cuisine Full of Wisdom and Nature

Contents

Introduction to Korean Food

KOREAN FOOD & FERMENTATION

One of the most interesting characteristics about Korean food is that the preparation of it often involves the process of fermentation. Fermentation was frequently utilized by enlightened spiritual practitioners of ancient Korea to create food that would benefit all people. In the old days, fermented food such as soy sauce (Ganjang), bean paste (Doenjang), and Korean chili pepper paste (Gochujang) were important source of protein for Koreans, and they remain popular to this day. Of course, no Korean meal would be complete without the ubiquitous kimchi, a fermented vegetable dish. Traditionally, fresh vegetables were scarce in winter. Kimchi, therefore, was the main source of vitamins for Koreans in wintertime.

Recently, the *Health* magazine announced the five best health foods in the world, and they included Greek yogurt, Spanish olive oil, Japanese natto, Indian lentils, and Korean kimchi. It is interesting to note that the three out of five healthiest foods are prepared through the process of fermentation. It begs the question: why is fermented food good for health? The process of fermentation brings about interesting changes to the flavor and texture of the food. More importantly, however, when food is fermented, it encourages the growth of healthy bacteria while preventing the growth of spoilage-causing bacteria. Doing this successfully requires special ingredients and carefully controlled conditions such as temperature and pH.

KOREAN FOOD AND DIET

According to the American Obesity Association (AOA), approximately 40 percent of Americans are overweight. It is a serious health problem for the nation since obesity is considered the second leading cause of preventable death in the United States. The most effective means of fighting obesity is to change one's eating habits. To that end, Korean diet has gained popularity in the United States, and many experts look to Korean food for their answer to fighting obesity. For example, the *Health* magazine credits kimchi as the "diet that has kept obesity at bay" in Korea and praises its health benefits. The Chair of the AOA is said to frequently enjoy eating kimchi and doenjang. We can attribute the benefits of Korean diet to the enlightened spiritual practitioners of ancient times, who were wise enough to realize the benefits of fermentation.

White Rice (Bap)

Ingredients
1.3 lb rice, water (1.2-1.4 times the volume of rice)

Recipe
▌ Rinse the rice in cold water to wash off dust and rice bran. Soak it in water for about 30 minutes.

▌ For newly harvested rice, less water (about 1.2 times the volume of rice) should be added. For aged rice, more water (1.5 times the volume of rice) should be used.

▌ Once the rice is cooked, let it sit for about 10 minutes. The rice becomes fully cooked through this process. When rice is cooked the best tasting rice is located in the middle. It should be evenly mixed with rice from other parts of the pot.

Rice with Mixed Vegetables (Bibimbap)

Ingredients

beef, bellflower root(doraji), braken(gosari), soybean sprouts, zucchini, mushrooms, rice, gochujang sauce, soy sauce, sesame oil, minced garlic, chopped scallion, sesame seeds, black pepper

Recipe

Beef: 1/4 lb lean beef cut in thin strips, 1 tsp soy sauce, 1 tsp sesame oil, 1 tsp minced garlic, 1 tsp chopped scallion, 1 tsp toasted sesame seeds, 1/4 tsp black pepper

Tip: You can use the bulgogi recipe on page 21.

▌Combine beef with the seasonings and quickly stir-fry over high heat and set aside.

Bellflower Root (doraji): 1/4 lb Bellflower root (cleaned, torn in thin strips), 1 tsp sesame oil, 1 tsp finely chopped scallion, 1/2 tsp finely minced garlic, 1 tsp toasted sesame seeds

▌Rub bellflower strips with salt, rinse, blanch in boiling water, squeeze out liquid, mix with seasoning and quickly stir fry over high heat and set aside.

Bracken (gosari): 1/4 lb precooked gosari (cut in 2-inch lengths), 1 tsp sesame oil, 1 tsp finely chopped scallion, 1 tsp toasted sesame seeds

▌Rinse the gosari, squeeze liquid out, mix with the seasonings, quickly stir-fry over high heat and set aside.

Soybean Sprouts: 1/4 lb cooked soybean sprouts (liquid squeezed out), 1 tsp sesame oil, 1 tsp soy sauce, 1 tsp finely chopped scallion, 1 tsp toasted sesame seeds

▌Combine the soybean sprouts with the seasonings and set aside.

Zucchini: 1 Zucchini (halved lengthwise and sliced), 1 tsp salt, 1 tsp sesame oil, 1 tsp toasted sesame seeds

▌Blanch the zucchini in boiling water, squeeze out liquid, and mix with the seasonings and set aside.

Mushrooms: 4 dried Pyogo a/k/a Shiitake mushrooms (softened in warm water and cut in strips), 1 tsp sesame oil, 1 tsp soy sauce, 1 tsp finely chopped scallion, 1 tsp toasted sesame seeds

▌Mix the mushrooms with the seasonings, quickly stir-fry over high heat and set aside.

Rice: 4 cups cooked rice, 1 tsp sesame oil

▌Combine the rice, sesame oil and salt and put 1 cup in each individual servings bowl.

Gochujang Sauce: 4 tsp gochujang, 1 tsp sugar, 1 tsp toasted sesame seeds, 2 tsp sesame oil

▌Combine all the ingredients in a bowl. Mix well.

Beauty of Bibimbap

Bibimbap is unique in that a variety of ingredients are mixed into one bowl. The beauty of bibimbap is in the perfect harmony between various tastes and nutrition that results from mixing many ingredients into one bowl. When different ingredients are mixed together, it is easier to eat one or two ingredients that you may not like.

According to Professor Mi-suk Lee at Seoul Women's University, the best thing about bibimbap is that it has all the five major food groups. In addition, most of the fat in bibimbap is vegetable fat.

James Philips of World Health Organization, as he was eating bibimbap, said to Korean reporters that in order to prevent obesity, Koreans should protect their traditional diet and not be influenced by fast food.

Bean Paste Stew (Doenjang jjigae)

Ingredients

1 Tsp doenjang, 3 dried Pyogo a/k/a Shiitake mushrooms, 1/2 potato, 2 green hot peppers, 1/4 bean curd(dubu)

Kelp Soup Base: 1 sheet of dry kelp (3"x3"), 3-4 dried anchovies, 1.7 oz Korean radish, 3 garlic cloves, 1/2 scallion, 1/2 onion, 3 cups of water

Recipe

▌Put the kelp soup base in the pot and boil. When it boils, add bean curd and potato.
▌Add doenjang and when it boils, add green hot peppers, Pyogo mushrooms.

Bean Paste Soup (Deonjang guk)

Recipe

Use the kelp soup base and add 5 oz of napa cabbage (baechu) leaves. Add adequate doenjang and sea salt to taste.

How Doenjang (fermented bean paste) Was First Made

There lived an enlightened master in ancient Korea, around the period of ancient Joseon (2333 BCE-108 BCE) to be more exact. He always pondered about how people might commit less sin. He concluded that people committed sins because their minds were not at ease. With this realization, he wondered if there were any food that could calm the minds of the people and help them realize the grace of the Heavens, so that they would commit less sin just by their habit of eating. Through his devoted prayers and meditation, he realized that he should use soybeans to create this special food since soybeans were very nutritious. He first soaked the soybeans in water for about a day and a half and let the soybeans simmer at low heat for roughly twelve hours. He then ground the soybeans and shaped them into blocks. These soybean blocks were hung from the eaves to be dried with sunlight and wind. By letting them receive the sunlight, he let the bean blocks absorb the energy of the Heavens. By letting them dry in the autumn wind, he meant to expose the bean blocks to the breath of Buddha. After the blocks were dried, they were then fermented. When the fermentation was complete, they were put into water. By soaking them in water, he meant to soak them in the mind of Buddha. Finally, the salt was added to the whole thing, which added the energy of the sea.

Doenjang was thus created with an enlightened master's compassionate and selfless wish to help people commit less sin. Because doenjang contains the energy of the heaven, sea, and Buddha, it fills people with these energies and puts their internal organs at ease. When the internal organs are at ease, people's minds are at ease. That is why doenjang is such wonderful and complete food.

Anti-Cancer Function of Doenjang

Soybeans are often called the "meat from the field." Meat proteins can leave toxins such as ammonia, uric acid and fat in our blood. However, the protein and fat in soybeans can help prevent diseases such as stroke and lung cancer. Soybeans are abundant in nucleic acid and lecithin which slow down the aging process. Also, soybeans have plant sterol that blocks the small intestine from absorbing cholesterol. Soybeans, themselves, have no Vitamin C, but soybean sprouts are abundant in Vitamin C and aspartic acid.

Researchers are beginning to realize that beans such as soybeans have abundant anti-cancer nutrients. Dr. Paul Terry at Albert Einstein Cancer Center wrote in Cancer International Journal that folic acid from beans could reduce the chance of contracting colon cancer. And Dr. Stefan Burners of University of Alabama stated that the mouse fed with beans had 70% lower incidence of lung cancer than the mouse fed with just grains.

Doenjang is made from fermenting soybeans. Its nutritional value is, therefore, much higher than plain soybeans. Professor Gun-young Park of Busan University, Korea published that the potent anti-cancer properties of doenjang could prevent and, to some extent fight cancer. Professor Park reported that extracts from doenjang could eradicate carcinogenic substances from one's body. According to his research, eating doenjang soup everyday could reduce the chance of getting cancer by 30 percent.

Spicy Beef Soup (Yukgaejang)

Ingredients

10 oz brisket, 3 oz bracken (gosari), 3 oz soybean sprout, 4 scallions, 2 Tbs Korean chili pepper powder, 1 Tbs minced garlic, 2 tsp sesame seed oil, 2 Tsp salt, 1 Tsp soy sauce, 3 eggs, 1/8 black pepper

Recipe

▌Boil dried gosari for 30 minutes or until tender.

▌Clean soybean sprouts. Cut scallions into similar length strips.

▌Pour 10 cups of water into a large pot and place the meat into the pot. Bring to a boil.

▌Reduce heat and simmer for at least one hour to make beef base. Remove the meat from the broth. Skim the fat and foam from the broth.

▌Once the meat has cooled, shred it into thin strips. Set aside.

▌In a large bowl, combine the garlic, Korean chili pepper powder, soy sauce and salt. Add the beef and mix thoroughly. Cover and let it sit for about 10 minutes.

▮ Combine the eggs and sesame oil in a small bowl and beat until well mixed.
▮ Bring the broth to a boil again. Add the seasoned meat, scallions and black pepper.
▮ Bring to a boil again, and then add the egg mix, drizzling it slowly over the boiling broth.
▮ Serve it with a bowl of rice and any other side dishes.

Nutrients in Soybean Sprouts

Because soybeans use stored starches and sugars to produce green shoots called sprouts, sprouted beans have less carbohydrates than the beans from which they grow. But Soybean sprouts are a good source of dietary fiber, including insoluble cellulose and lignin in the leaf portion and soluble pectin and gums in the bean.

Soybean sprout helps people recover from a hangover quickly. The roots of the sprouts have lots of asparagine that reduces the acetaldehyde, which is formed after drinking alcohol. Soybean sprouts are also high in the B Vitamin folate and Vitamin C.

Raw beans contain anti-nutrient chemicals that inhibit the enzymes we use to digest proteins and starches; hemagglutinens (substances that make red blood cells clump together); and "factors" that may inactivate vitamin A. These chemicals are usually destroyed when the beans are heated.

Hot Spicy Fish Soup (Maeuntang)

Ingredients

One 12-16 oz red snapper or cod fish (any meaty white-fleshed fish will do), head and tail removed, cut into thirds and gutted, a handful of littleneck clams or mussels, 1/4 of a large Korean radish, 1/2 zucchini, 1/2 onion, a handful of crown daisy, 1 small bag of Paengi a/k/a Enoki mushrooms, 1/2 block of firm bean curd, 2 scallions (both white and green parts), 1 Korean chili pepper, 1 green hot pepper

Kelp base soup: 20 anchovies, 1 sheet of kelp (4"x4"), 8 cups of water

Seasoning: 3-1/2 large spoonful of hot Korean chili pepper powder, 5 large spoonful of kelp soup base, 1 spoonful minced garlic, 2 large spoonfuls of salted and fermented shrimp sauce (saeujeot)

16

▌Remove the fish pieces from the plastic bag and give them a quick rinse under cold tap water, making sure to clean out the insides (especially any dark bloody bits that cling to the fish bones, as those tend to coagulate in the soup, not really adding to the flavor).

▌Put kelp base soup with the radish that has been cut into 1/4" quarter-moon slices. (Make sure to remove the outer peel of the radish).

▌When it boils, add the seasoning, zucchini (1/3"-1/2" half-moons) and onion.

▌When it boils again, add fish (Please do not cover the pot, while it boils with fish). Add the clams and/or mussels at this point.

▌Add crown daisy, Paengi mushrooms, cubed bean curd, cut-up scallions, Korean chili pepper and green pepper.

▌Add a bit more water or fermented shrimp sauce (saeujeot) to your taste.

▌Boil for 2-3 minutes; lower the heat to a simmer for another 4-5 minutes (or until ready to serve).

Steamed Bean Curd Mixed with Beef, Various Vegetables and Mushrooms (Dubuseon)

Ingredients

1 block water packed bean curd (dubu), 1.4 oz ground beef or chicken breast, 2 pyogo a/k/a shiitake mushrooms, 4 seogi mushrooms (manna lichen), 1 egg, 1 tsp pine nuts, 2 tsp salt, 1 tsp sugar, 1 Tsp chopped scallion, 1/2 Tsp minced garlic, 1 tsp sesame oil, 1 tsp toasted sesame seeds, black pepper (to your taste)

Mustard Vinegar Sauce: 5 Tsp mustard powder, 2 1/2 Tsp warm water, 1 Tsp pine nuts, 3 Tsp sugar, 3 Tsp vinegar, 1/4 tsp soy sauce, 3 Tsp Korean pear juice, *1/3 tsp citron honey concentrate, a pinch of salt

Garnish (Jidan): Separate the egg yolk from the white and pan-fry the yolk and white and cut them in 1-inch length.

* marked ingredient is optional.

▌Squeeze water from bean curd and finely chop or mince the beef or chicken breast.

▌Allow dried pyogo mushrooms to be soaked in cold water for 24 hours. Cut pyogo and seogi mushrooms in thin slices.

▌Cut shredded Korean chili pepper into 1-inch length. Cut pine nuts in half.

▌Mix the minced bean curd with meat and add the seasoning and mix well.

▌Place a wet cheese cloth in the steamer and spread the seasoned bean curd into 0.4 inch thick pieces. Place the mushrooms, garnish, shredded Korean chili pepper, pine nuts on top of the bean curd and steam for 10 minutes.

▌Let it cool, and cut it into squares and serve with the mustard sauce.

The Origin of Dubu and Soybean Sprout

About 3,000 years ago, there was a young spiritual practitioner who was attending to an enlightened teacher. Due to his old age, his teacher could not chew very well. To feed his aged teacher, the disciple would chew the rice for him instead. The disciple realized that despite his efforts, he was swallowing most of the nutrition for himself. He felt terrible that he was taking in the nutrition that was meant for his teacher. He fervently searched for food that his teacher could eat. As he was wise, he soon realized that soybeans were very nutritious. His first attempt was to grind the soybeans and boil them.

Eventually, dubu was invented from his efforts. The excess soybeans that were put into storage occasionally became wet. The wet soybeans grew sprouts, and that is how we came to have soybean sprouts. The young practitioner taught people how to make dubu and soybean sprouts.

Pan-Fried Bean Curd with Soy Sauce (Dubujeon)

Ingredients

1 lb block medium firm bean curd, 2 eggs, 1/4 tsp salt, 1 tsp vegetable oil, 2 tsp soy sauce, 1 1/2 tsp sesame oil, 1 1/2 tsp Korean chili pepper powder, or more or less to taste, 2 tsp thinly sliced scallions, 1 1/2 tsp toasted sesame seeds

Recipe

▌Slice the bean curd into 6 pieces and lay them out on paper towels to drain while you prepare the rest of the ingredients.

▌Beat the eggs with the salt and set aside. Combine the sauce ingredients.

▌Heat the vegetable oil in a large, preferably non-stick frying pan over medium heat.

▌Dip the bean curd slices in the egg mixture and place them in a pan. Pour the remaining egg mixture over the bean curd. Fry until golden brown on one side, then flip over and cook until golden brown on the other side.

▌Transfer to a plate and drizzle with the sauce.

Tip: You can use parboiled bean curd instead of pan-fried ones.

Bulgogi

Ingredients

1 lb beef, sliced as thin as possible, 5 or 6 mid-size mushrooms (button mushroom), 1/2 of onion (add it when pan-frying)

Marinating Sauce: 4 Tsp Korean pear juice, 1 Tsp red wine, 1 1/2 Tsp honey or sugar, 4 Tsp dark soy sauce, 2 Tsp chopped scallions, 2 Tsp minced garlic, 1 Tsp sesame oil, a pinch of black pepper

Recipe

▎Cut beef into mouth-size pieces. Put meat into a strainer and sprinkle water to remove blood.

▎Mix pear juice and red wine into a bowl. Add beef to the wine and pear juice mix and marinate while preparing the marinating sauce.

▎Mix dark soy sauce and honey in a bowl and stir until the honey completely dissolves. Add scallions, garlic, sesame oil and black pepper to the dark soy sauce and honey mix. Add the soy sauce and honey marinade to the meat submerged in wine and pear juice and let it marinate for 12 hours.

▎Pan-fry the marinated beef.

Bulgogi, Marinated Meat: Health Benefits

Americans usually like to grill their beef, which produces the cholesterol oxidation products (COPs) that cause heart disease or cancer as it is cooked. However, according to a recent news article, marinating meat with soy sauce and sugar inhibits the formation of COPs. Dr. Bing-Huei Chen and his colleagues at Fu Jen University in Taipei carried out the research, and their findings were published in the *Journal of Agricultural and Food Chemistry* (June 28, 2006). Dr. Chen's experiments were performed on eggs and pork, because these are very commonly eaten in China. When we apply the same result to bulgogi, we can see the health benefits of it. Unrefined brown sugar and soy sauce are used as a marinade for bulgogi. Using unrefined brown sugar instead of refined white sugar is better for the health.

In addition, the Korean pear extract makes the meat tender. By decomposing protein and fat enzymes, it makes the meat taste better, and also easier to digest. On the other hand, using kiwi and/or pineapple does not achieve the same result as using the Korean pear extract. When we marinate and ferment the meat for 12 hours with pineapple or kiwi extract, the meat loses cohesiveness because kiwi and pineapple make the meat overly tender. Only those who do not understand the fermentation process of marinating will recommend using kiwi or pineapple for bulgogi.

Braised Short Rib Stew (Galbijjim)

Ingredients

2.2 lbs beef short rib, English or "thick" cut (galbi)

A. 1 1/2 cup water, 1/4 cup cooking rice wine, *2/3 cup oligosaccharides, 1/2 cup soy sauce

B. 3/4 onion, 1/2 Korean pear, 2 Tsp ginger, 1/3 cup minced garlic, 2/3 Tsp whole ungrounded black pepper, 1 piece of scallion, 3 dried Korean peppers, *1 piece of Hedysarum (Sweetvetch), *1-2 Liquorice (the root of Glycyrrhiza glabra, from which a sweet flavor can be extracted), *1 piece of castor aralia (Kalopanax) bark

C. 5.3 oz Korean white radish, 5.3 oz carrots, 10 chestnuts, 10 gingko nuts, 7 dried Pyogo a/k/a Shiitake mushrooms, 8 daechu (dates or jujubes), 1 Tsp sesame oil

* marked ingredients are optional.

23

▌Remove fat from the short ribs and soak in cold water for at least one hour (Change water once or twice).

▌Parboil the short ribs. Place the short ribs in a strainer and pour cold water to remove impurities from the short ribs (If the meat is over 4.4 lbs, soak the pre-cooked short ribs in cold water for about a day to remove blood).

▌Put the ingredients listed in paragraph B into a mesh bag (made out of cotton or cheesecloth).

▌Put ingredients listed in paragraph A and the cheese cloth bag into a pot and boil at high heat. When it boils over, reduce the heat to medium and continue to boil until the short ribs are fully cooked (about 2 hours).

▌Cut the Korean white radish and carrots into fan-shaped pieces. Score the small dried Pyogo mushrooms by making cross-shaped shallow cuts into the mushrooms.

▌Put the ingredients listed in paragraph C with fully cooked short ribs and some ribs broth. Braise until very little broth remains. Add sesame oil.

Chicken-Ginseng Soup (Samgyetang)

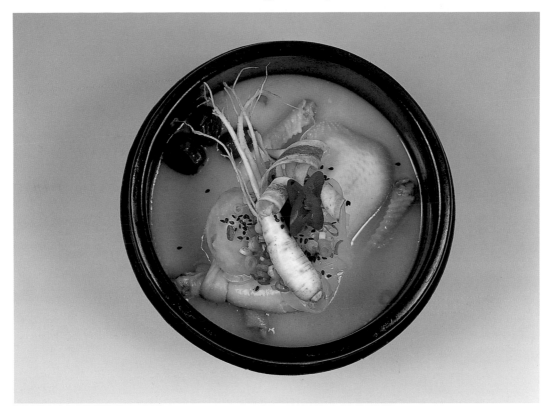

Ingredients

1 Cornish Hen (about 1 3/4 lbs) cavity well cleaned, 1 tsp salt, 4 cups water, 2 1/2 tsp glutinous rice (soaked in water 20-30 minutes, drained), 4 dried daechu (dates or jujubes), 3 cloves garlic, 4 chestnuts (peeled), 8 gingko nuts, 14 cups beef broth, *1 slice licorice root, 1/4 tsp salt, 1/4 tsp black pepper, 1 fresh ginseng root (small roots trimmed, peeled)

* marked ingredient is optional.

Recipe

▌Soak the hen in 4 cups of water with 1 tsp salt for 30 minutes. Remove and dry the cavity.

▌Mix the rice, daechu, garlic, chestnuts, gingko nuts and ginseng. Stuff the hen's cavity, securing the opening with twine or poultry skewers.

▌Put the hen in a pot, pour in the beef broth, add the licorice root and cook 30 minutes. Skim off any froth that forms during cooking.

▌Discard licorice, season with salt and pepper and boil about 10 minutes more.

▌Serve with whole chicken in a deep bowl.

Food as Medicine

There is a saying in Korea that the food that we eat everyday is the medicine that invigorates us. In Korea, there are wild ginsengs that grow in the mountains called Sansam. Because these Sansams absorb the bright energy and the essence of the mountains as they grow, they are known to cure even cancer. Sansams, however, are very rare and hard to find. That is why people farm Insams, or ginsengs. The quality of Insam farmed in Japan or China is not as good as the one farmed in Korea. Because the earth's energy in Korea is different from that of Japan or China, the quality of Insam cannot be the same.

People who are ill or lack energy can sometimes recover from their illness by eating vegetables or herbs from deep within the mountains. These herbs and vegetables, therefore, can be an important medicine for them.

We add milk vetch roots and licorice roots to galbijjim. These are also medicinal herbs that grow in the mountains. By adding these, we can remove the smell of meat and make it tastier. They are also good for the body.

Royal Braised Chicken (Gungjung dakjjim)

Ingredients

1 whole chicken, 2 Tsp onion juice, 2 Tsp jeongjong (refined rice wine), 2 cloves garlic, 1/2 scallion, 1 Korean chili pepper

Sauce: 4 Tsp soy sauce, 1 Tsp oyster sauce, 3 Tsp sugar, 2 Tsp minced garlic, 1/2 Tsp minced ginger, 2 Tsp Jeongjong (refined rice wine), 2 Tsp cooking rice wine, *2/3 Tsp red hot pepper powder, 1/4 tsp black pepper, 1 Tsp sesame oil, 12 chestnuts, 8 daechu (dates or jujubes) 4 pyogo a/k/a Shiitake mushrooms, 1/2 onion, 1 Tsp cooking oil, a pinch of salt

* marked ingredient is optional.

Recipe

▌Clean the chicken by scraping it with salt, and cut it into 2-3 inch pieces. Slice garlic and cut scallion into 1-inch length pieces. Slice Korean chili pepper and remove pepper seeds.

▌Heat the cooking oil in the pan. Put garlic, scallion and Korean chili pepper in the pan first, and add chicken.

▌Cook until chicken turns to brown and add water until chicken is fully submerged. Boil about 30 minutes and while boiling remove foam.

▌Cut onion into appropriate size and cut mushrooms in 4 pieces. Peel the chestnuts and soak in cold water. Clean daechu by scrubbing in water and peeling the flesh off the seed.

▌When the chicken boils, add onion, chestnuts, daechu and mushrooms. Add sauce. Let it simmer with the sauce.

Chicken Salad with Mustard Sauce
(Dakgogi Naengchae)

Ingredients

1/2 lbs chicken breast, 1 Tsp onion juice, 1 Tsp white wine, 1 tsp sesame oil, a pinch of salt and white pepper, 1/2 Korean pear, 1/2 cucumber, 5 daechu (dates or jujubes), *1 root ginseng, *1/2 bamboo shoot 3 chestnuts, a pinch of salt

Mustard Vinegar Sauce: 5 Tsp mustard powder, 2 1/2 Tsp warm water, 1 Tsp pine juice, 3 Tsp sugar, 3 Tsp vinegar, 1/4 tsp soy sauce, 3 Tsp Korean pear juice, *1/3 tsp citron honey concentrate, a pinch of salt   * marked ingredients are optional.

Recipe

❚Prepare 1/2 lbs of chicken breast and add onion juice, white wine, sesame oil, salt and pepper. Steam chicken breast for 20 minutes and let it cool. Cut chicken into 2 inch pieces.

❚Cut pear in half and remove seeds. Cut it into 1-inch length and 0.4-inch width pieces. Slice cucumber and sprinkle with salt. Squeeze water out. Peel the daechu flesh off the seed and cut it into four pieces. Peel the chestnuts and slice them into thin pieces.

❚Grind pine nuts and mix it with mustard sauce, salt, garlic, sugar and vinegar. Cool in the refrigerator and mix with mustard sauce right before serving.

Kimchi

Ingredients

4 large napa cabbages (baechu), 2 white Korean radish (mu), 21 oz sea salt, 1 cup rice powder, 1 cup fish sauce, i.e. anchovy-based broth (jeotgal), 1/2 cup salted shrimps, 2 cups Korean chili pepper powder, 1/2 cup minced garlic, 2 Tsp minced ginger, 14 oz scallion, 2 chopped onions, 1 Korean pear, *honey powder

* marked ingredient is optional.

Recipe

▌Remove the outer leaves of the cabbage that are not fresh. Cut the cabbage in half (lengthwise) from the bottom of the cabbage, but cut only about 1/4 way in. Then, split the remaining portion of the cabbage in half by hand. If the initial cut is too deep, it may cause the leaves inside to fall off when you wash and salt the cabbage.

▌Prepare salt solution (about 8%-10% salt) in a large bucket.

▌Soak the cut cabbages in the salt solution. Scatter a little bit of sea salt inside the cabbages. Place the cabbages facing up in a bucket for about 12 hours. During the salting process, turn over the cabbages once or twice so that the cabbages are salted evenly.

29

▌Rinse the salted cabbages several times with fresh water. Place the cabbages in a large basket that could function as a strainer. Make sure that the cut surface of the cabbages is facing down so that extra water from the cabbages is drained.

White Korean Radish: Wash and cut the radish into finger length strips (The size and length may vary from types of kimchi).

Rice Porridge: Mix 1 cup of rice powder with 3 cups of water and boil the mixture at low heat. Let it cool once it is boiled.

Korean Chili Pepper Powder: Soak the powder in warm water

Scallion: Cut scallions into 1.5-2 inch length pieces.

▌Mince and chop garlic, ginger, onion and Korean pear.
▌Evenly mix the rice porridge, fish sauce, Korean red chili pepper powder, minced garlic, ginger, onion and Korean pear in a large bucket and add cut radish and scallion.
▌Put an adequate amount of the seasoning mix between every single cabbage leaf. Fold the cabbages in half (lengthwise) and, using the outer leaf, wrap the cabbage so that the seasoning will not leak. Neatly lay the cabbage wraps inside a container. Let the kimchi sit for 4-6 weeks underground (in temperature ranging from 0-5°C).

Tip: Usually, we keep raw kimchi for 2 days in room temperature and have it refrigerated afterwards. The best way to make well-fermented and delicious kimchi is to keep the kimchi inside a kimchi refrigerator. To eat gimjang kimchi (kimchi prepared for winter) until next spring, add more salt to the saline solution.

The Origin of Kimchi

In ancient Korea, there lived a young spiritual practitioner who studied under an enlightened master and attended to the needs of his teacher. In order to serve food to his teacher, he raised crops in the field and gathered wild fruits from the mountains. He was so devoted to his teacher that his sole wish was to serve his teacher well.

He knew that radish was very nutritious and thought about how he could use radish to prepare food for his teacher. He cut the radish into thin slices at first. He soaked them in water and added salt. He then floated flower petals on the water. His attempt to soak them in water just produced sharp and bitter taste for the radish. Then he tried salting the slices of radish first, but it did not taste good either. Finally, he put them in an earthen jar and let it sit for about 20 days to a month, fermenting it. That was how kimchi first came into existence. People later put more flavor to it and used cabbage to make various types of kimchi.

Kimchi's Nutritional Benefit

Many nutrition experts have deemed kimchi to be one of the top health foods in the world. Kimchi is prepared by fermenting vegetables that are seasoned with Korean chili pepper, garlic, green onion, ginger, and other ingredients. Kimchi contains a large amount of vitamin C and beta carotene, as well as substantial amounts of protein, calcium, and vitamins A, B1 and B2. Well-fermented kimchi contains healthy bacteria that suppresses the growth of harmful bacteria and protects the body from diseases. Health experts have reported that kimchi may prevent SARS (Severe Acute Respiratory Syndrome) and may also function as a potential guardian against the Avian Bird Flu Pandemic. According to a BBC report, scientists in Seoul declared that 11 of 13 infected chickens started to recover from the avian flu after being fed an extract of kimchi.

Last year, KAERI (Korea Atomic Energy Research Institute) entered an agreement with the NASA Food Technology Commercial Space Center to develop "Space Kimchi." In zero gravity, the air does not move and astronauts cannot smell, so their sense of taste, too, is dramatically reduced. Space kimchi is expected to be of great help in stimulating astronauts' appetite with its zest and spices. In addition, it is effective in promoting the intestinal functions, which tend to be somewhat sluggish in space, with abundant fiber.

Taste of Kimchi: Transcending the Five Tastes

The Chinese version of kimchi is called zu and the Japanese osinko. The Chinese and Japanese kimchi are just cabbages pickled in salt.

They, therefore, taste like nothing more than vegetables pickled in salt. Because the vegetables become limp, they lose the fresh crispiness.

Although Korean kimchi shares the similar ingredients with the Chinese and Japanese version of kimchi, the hot pepper in Korean kimchi causes a chemical change that, in turn, creates an entirely different food from the Chinese or Japanese version of pickled vegetable. Sprinkling hot pepper powder on osinko will not transform it into Korean kimchi, and removing all the hot pepper powder from Korean kimchi will not turn it into Chinese zu.

Koreans at that time were able to create a revolutionary food product using just hot pepper. What makes it so revolutionary?

First, no other food in the world can recreate the savory fermented taste of kimchi. In the West, a taste is characterized under five categories, i.e. salty, sweet, bitter, sour and spicy. There is no category for the sixth taste, or the savory fermented taste. It is said that the human tongue has taste receptors for five types of taste. Perhaps, the sixth taste receptor is not well developed for the people outside of Korea.

Right before kimchi goes bad, it attains this fermented flavor. The capsaicin from Korean chili pepper is the chemical agent that preserves this flavor which also prevents kimchi from going bad. Vegetables can easily lose their freshness and, for thousands of years, the mankind has been trying to preserve the freshness of vegetables for their diet. Our ancestors achieved this dream with the help of Korean chili pepper. Because of the Korean chili pepper, kimchi can retain its crispy freshness even after several months. Even though they did not know how to perform quantitative or qualitative analysis of different ingredients, they were able to unleash the power of capsaicin hidden in a Korean chili pepper. We can only be astonished at their wisdom.

The reputation of kimchi has spread to the rest of the world and pleased the palates of many people. The words, "ondol" and "kimchi," are included in the revised Oxford Dictionary. People can now buy kimchi at the grocery stores in the suburbs of Brussels or in Nairobi. Kimchi has indeed become a part of international cuisine.

The research on kimchi has become international as well. A few years ago, the researchers at Kyoto University in Japan discovered that kimchi has high capacity to break down fat due to its capsaicin. What is really amazing is that eating a Korean chili pepper alone will not achieve the same result. Only when the Korean chili pepper is fermented within kimchi, does it bring out the ability to break down fat.

The more people eat meat, the more fat is accumulated in the body. The accumulation of fat is not only a cause of obesity but also a cause of many adult diseases. Recently, gallstone disease has increased among Koreans. Doctors say that when Koreans did not eat much meat, the gallstones of Koreans were usually dark in color. But as the fat intake increased, the color of gallstones has become whiter. The most powerful weapon against fat, which even changes the color of gallstones, can be found in Korean food. In the old days, our ancestors always ate pork with kimchi and added kimchi to soups that had pork. We can only marvel at their wisdom.

Kimchi Fried Rice (Kimchi bokkeumbap)

Ingredients

3 tsp sesame oil, 1 cup chopped kimchi, 1/4 cup kimchi juice, 2-3 cups cooked white rice (leftover rice works great), 1 tsp toasted sesame seeds

Recipe

In a large pot, put sesame oil and add kimchi and rice. Simmer for 20 minutes stirring occasionally and add kimchi juice. Add the sesame seeds and mix all the ingredients together.

Kimchi Stew (Kimchi jjigae)

Ingredients

1/2 lb lean pork or 1 can of tuna, adjust according to preference (more meat than kimchi or vise versa), 2 cups kimchi, 1 Tsp sesame oil, 1 Tsp Korean chili pepper paste, 1 Tsp minced garlic, *4 Pyogo a/k/a Shiitake mushrooms, 1 block water packed bean curd, 2 scallions, 1 onion

* marked ingredient is optional.

Recipe

▌Cut pork in bite-size chunks or strips. Cut kimchi into 1 inch pieces.

▌In a pot, add the pork, sesame oil, Korean chili pepper paste and minced garlic. Stir and cook over a medium high heat until the pork is nearly cooked through.

▌Add kimchi, some kimchi juice and 3 cups water. Bring to boil.

▌In the meantime, cut the mushrooms, bean curd and scallions. Lower the heat, and add the remaining ingredients. Let it simmer for 1-2 minutes until bean curd is heated through.

▌Serve immediately.

Kimchi Pancake (Kimchijeon)

Ingredients

1 1/2 cups all-purpose flour, 1/2 cup water, 1 egg, 10 oz chopped kimchi (preferably aged), 1/4 cup kimchi juice, 4 oz scallions (finely minced using the greener parts), 2 green hot peppers (sliced, optional), vegetable oil for cooking

Dipping Sauce: 2 tsp soy sauce, 1/2 tsp Korean chili pepper powder,1 tsp sesame seeds, 1/2 tsp rice vinegar

Recipe

▌Combine the flour with the water and egg and mix.
▌Add kimchi, kimchi juice, scallions and peppers.
▌Using 1 tsp of vegetable oil, cook 1 thin pancake at a time over a medium flame. The batter will make 4 pancakes.

Kimchi Soup with Rice (Kimchi gukbap)

Ingredients

10.5 oz kimchi, 2 1/2 cups white rice (left over will be good), 1 piece of laver, 1/3 scallion, soy sauce, a dash of salt and black pepper, 5 cups anchovy broth, 1 Korean chili pepper, 1 green hot pepper, 1 egg

Anchovy Broth: Boil for 30 minutes 10 anchovies and 6 cups water

Recipe

▌Cut kimchi into 1-inch length pieces, and slice scallion diagonally. Slice Korean chili pepper and green hot pepper.

▌Mix anchovy broth with kimchi and add soy sauce and salt to your taste.

▌When it boils, add rice and scallion. Add Korean chili pepper, green pepper, laver and egg.

Spicy Stir-Fired Octopus with Vegetables
(Nakji bokkeum)

Ingredients

1 lb octopus (squid can be used as a substitute), 1/2 onion (sliced to make o-rings), 2 Korean peppers (sliced on the bias), 2 scallions (sliced on the bias), 1/4 carrot, thin sliced 1 green hot pepper (sliced in long strips), *4 Pyogo a/k/a Shiitake mushrooms

* marked ingredient is optional.

Sauce: 2 1/2 tsp gochujang (Korean chili pepper paste), 2 tsp Korean chili pepper powder, 1 tsp soy sauce, 2 tsp sesame oil, 1 tsp sesame seeds, 2 tsp minced garlic

Recipe

▌Wash and rinse octopus, cut the legs into 2"-3" length pieces, open head and take out inside, quarter the head. Drain well. Prepare and mix all ingredients for sauce.

▌Combine final sauce with octopus and marinate for 10 minutes.

▌Heat pan on a medium high heat, cook for 8-10 minutes or until done.

Braised Sea Bream Seasoned in Spicy Soy Sauce (Domi jorim)

Ingredients

1 sea bream, 1 Tsp salt, dash of white pepper, 4 Tsp white wine, 1 Tsp lemon juice, 4 cups beef broth, 1/2 cup soy sauce, 1/3 cup sugar, 1 Tsp ginger juice, 1/2 cup cooking wine, 1 scallion, 4 cloves garlic, 1 Korean chili pepper, 1 piece ginger

Recipe

▌Scale and clean the sea bream. Make cross-shaped shallow cuts on the sea bream and sprinkle white pepper, salt. Add white wine and lemon juice to the sea bream.

▌Heat the pan and fry the sea bream. Do not fully cook.

▌Add all the ingredients in a frying pan and cover the pan with foil. Make a couple of holes in the cover. Let it simmer.

▌When it boils over, reduce the heat to medium and continue to boil until the sea bream is fully cooked.

▌Garnish with scallion and garlic on the fully cooked sea bream.

Prawn with Pine Nut Dressing (Daeha jajjeup muchim)

4 prawns, 1 piece of lemon, 1 square inch kelp, 1 cucumber, 3.5 oz bamboo shoot, 1/4 Korean pear, 1 tsp salt, a dash of white pepper, 1 tsp white wine

Pine Nut Dressing: 6 Tsp ground pine nuts, 4 Tsp lemon juice, 1 tsp sesame oil, a dash of white pepper

▌Clean and devein prawns and boil with lemon, kelp and salt (Prawn must be boiled from cold water. It makes the prawn soft). Let it cool. Shell and halve them lengthwise. Add salt, white pepper and white wine to prawns.

▌Slice cucumber in half-moon shape and pickle cucumber with 1 tsp salt, 2 Tsp vinegar and 1 Tsp sugar. Squeeze cucumber and drain water. Slice bamboo shoot diagonally and soak in cold water and drain. Slice Korean pear in the same shape as cucumber. Mix cucumber, bamboo shoot and pear with 2/3 of prepared pine nut dressing.

▌Place prawns around the dish and put the mixed cucumber, bamboo shoot and pear in the middle. Sprinkle the remaining pine nut sauce over prawns.

Seafood and Scallion Pancake (Haemul pajeon)

Ingredients

7 oz fresh squid (calamari), 18 oz fresh shrimp, 2 oz oysters, 2 cups all-purpose flour, 1 1/2 cups water, 2 eggs, 1/2 tsp salt, 5 oz scallions (chopped into 1-inch pieces), 2 tsp vegetable oil

Dipping Sauce: 2 tsp soy sauce, 2 tsp vinegar, 1 tsp sugar, 1 tsp Korean chili pepper powder, 2 tsp sesame seeds

Recipe

▌Clean all seafood and slice thin. Set aside.

▌In a mixing bowl, combine the flour, water, and eggs. Mix the ingredients in a massaging motion. Add the shrimp, squid, and salt. Add these ingredients to the batter and mix well. Add the oysters and scallions and mix.

▌Over a medium flame, heat 1/2 teaspoon of oil in a frying pan. When the pan is heated, spread the batter, thinly covering the whole pan. Heat until egg is cooked.

▌Continue this step until all batter is used.

▌Prepare the dipping sauce by mixing all the ingredients in a medium bowl.

Mung Bean Pancake (Nokdu bindaetteok)

Ingredients

1 cup dried peeled (yellow) mung beans, 2 medium carrots, 1 bunch scallions (white and pale green parts only), 1 (5-inch) fresh Korean chili pepper, thinly sliced crosswise, 1 tsp minced garlic, 1 cup water, 2 large eggs, 2 tsp all-purpose flour, 1 tsp salt, 4 tsp vegetable oil

Dipping Sauce: 3 tsp soy sauce, 2 tsp rice vinegar (not seasoned), 1 tsp toasted sesame seeds, 1/4 tsp Korean chili pepper powder, 1/4 tsp sesame oil

Recipe

▌ Rinse mung beans in a sieve under cold running water until water runs clear. Cover beans with cold water by 2 inches in a bowl and soak, chilled, at least 2 hours.

▌ Cut carrots into thin matchsticks, preferably using slicer. Halve scallions lengthwise and cut into 2-inch pieces. Combine carrots, scallions, pepper, and garlic in a large bowl.

▌ Drain mung beans and purée with water in a food processor until smooth, about 1 minute. Add eggs, flour, and salt and blend until smooth, about 30 seconds. Pour mixture over vegetables in bowl and stir with a flexible spatula (Batter will be thick).

▌Heat 1 tsp oil in a large heavy nonstick skillet (at least 8 inches across bottom) over moderate heat until hot but not smoking, then swirl to coat. Stir batter, then ladle 1 cup batter into skillet, pressing down lightly with a large spatula to flatten and evenly distribute vegetables, to make an 8-inch pancake (less than 1/2 inch thick).

▌Cook until edges begin to bubble and turn golden, 1-2 minutes, then turn over with spatula and cook until other side is golden, 1-2 minutes more. Transfer pancake to paper towels to drain.

▌Make 3 more pancakes in same manner, stacking them (after draining briefly) if desired.

▌Transfer pancakes, 1 at a time, to a cutting board and cut each into 6 wedges.

▌Serve warm or at room temperature with dipping sauce.

Pan-Fried Zucchini (Hobakjeon)

Ingredients

1/2 cup flour, 2 eggs (beaten), 1 tsp oil, 2 large zucchinis (cut into 1/4-inch slices)

Dipping Sauce: 3 tsp soy sauce, 3 tsp vinegar (optional), 1/4 tsp sesame seeds

Recipe

▌Place the flour in a bowl, and the beaten eggs in a shallow bowl.

▌Heat oil in a large non-stick skillet over medium-high heat.

▌Coat each zucchini slice with flour, then with the beaten egg mixture, and fry in pan for 5 minutes or until both sides are golden. Fill the pan just enough so you have space to flip them over.

▌Repeat as necessary.

▌Make dipping sauce with soy sauce and vinegar with sesame seeds, or soy sauce with sesame seeds only.

▌Serve hot or cold with dipping sauce on the side.

Pan-Fried Codfish Fillet (Daegujeon)

Ingredients

1 pound codfish fillets, 1 tsp salt, 1 tsp freshly ground black pepper, 1/2 cup all purpose flour, 2 eggs (egg white only), 2 tsp vegetable oil

Vinegar Soy Sauce : 2 tsp soy sauce, 2 tsp rice wine, 2 tsp rice vinegar or apple cider vinegar, 1 tsp sesame oil, 2 tsp freshly squeezed lemon juice, a pinch of salt, 1 tsp toasted sesame seeds, a pinch of freshly ground black pepper

Recipe

▌Rinse the fish and pat dry with a paper towel. Place it in a colander in a single layer. Add the salt and pepper. Set aside for 5 minutes.

▌Spread the flour on a small plate. In a shallow bowl, lightly beat the eggs with a few drops of water.

▌In a large nonstick skillet, heat 1/2 tsp vegetable oil over medium-high heat until very hot, but not smoking.

▌Divide the fish into four batches. Working with the first batch, dredge each piece with flour and coat with the egg.

▌Quickly add the fish to the skillet and cook for 2 minutes per side, or until the coating is golden, yet moist. Adjust the heat between medium and medium-high to keep the coating from becoming too brown and dry.

▌Transfer to a serving platter. Repeat three times with remaining batches of fish using 1/2 tsp of oil for each batch.

▌To serve, arrange fish on a platter in a fan pattern, garnishing with lemon and parsley. Serve with Vinegar Soy Sauce.

Art of Pan-Frying

Traditionally, Koreans preferred pan frying over deep frying. Since pan frying uses much less oil than deep frying, it is a healthier way of cooking. Jeon is a type of pancake prepared by pan frying different ingredients such as meat, fish or vegetables. The main ingredient is usually thinly coated in flour and egg before being fried on a pan. The name "Jeon" was derived from the word "pan fried flower." Pajeon is prepared by pan frying a variety of seafood mixed in with flour batter. The flour batter is usually fermented for a day. Pajeon is abundant in protein, Vitamins B2 and A. Also the greenish part of scallion has plenty of calcium.

Pumpkin Porridge (Hobakjuk)

Ingredients

1 lbs sweet Korean pumpkin, 4 cups glutinous rice flour, salt, water

Recipe

▌Wash the pumpkin and cut it into 4 pieces. Remove the seeds and place into a large pot, skins facing up.

▌Add water to cover the pumpkin pieces and bring to a boil. Boil for about 25 to 30 minutes, until pumpkin is soft.

▌Remove the pumpkin and let it cool. Scrape out the insides of the pumpkin with a wooden spoon or spatula.

▌Place the pumpkin back into the pot; add the rice flour and about 10 cups water.

▌Continue to cook over medium heat. Add salt as needed and continue cooking, stirring continuously to keep the porridge from sticking to the bottom of the pot.

▌Cook for about 30 minutes, and then turn off the heat and cover, letting it steam for another 10 minutes or so. Serve warm or at room temperature.

Pine Nut Porridge (Jajjuk)

Ingredients

1 cup rice, 1/2 cup pine nuts, 4 cups water, 1 daechu (dates or jujubes), salt

Recipe

▌Wash rice and soak it in water for more than 30 minutes. Clean pine nuts, and leave 6 pine nuts for decoration. Clean daechu and cut in the middle to take out the seed. Cut daechu into small pieces.

▌Pour rest of the pine nuts, soaked rice, and 1 cup of water into a blender, and grind them. Pour 1 more cup of water and grind.

▌Pour the mixture into a sauce pan with jujube. Place it on medium heat and keep stirring slowly with wooden spatula until the mixture becomes almost thick as ketchup. Add salt to taste.

▌Serve in a bowl and decorate with pine nuts.

Mixed Vegetables with Sweet Vermicelli Noodles (Japchae)

Ingredients

12 oz glass noodle, 5 oz beef, 5 Pyogo a/k/a Shiitake mushrooms, 1 carrot, 1 onion, 1 egg, 1/3 lbs spinach, 5 tsp oil, 2 tsp soy sauce, 1 tsp sugar, salt, sesame oil, toasted sesame seeds (pinch), 1 tsp minced garlic, 1 tsp chopped scallion, black pepper (pinch), 3 dried kelp pieces (4"x4")

Recipe

▌ Soak mushrooms in water for 15 minutes. Cut off stems. Cut mushrooms into thin strips.

▌ Cut beef into thin strips and marinate it with the mushrooms in a seasoning of: 2 tsp of soy sauce, 1 tsp of sugar, 1 tsp of minced garlic, 1 tsp of sesame seed oil, 1 tsp of chopped scallion, and a pinch of ground pepper. Cut carrots and onion into thin strips.

▌ Cook spinach in boiling water for about 2 minutes. Cool spinach in running water. Squeeze the water out of the spinach. Season the spinach slightly with salt and sesame oil.

▌ Fry the egg in a pan with a pinch of salt. Cut the egg into thin slices.

▌Cut the noodles into 10" length pieces. Soak in cold water for 10 minutes. Add 12 cups of water to a pot and boil dried kelp pieces to create kelp base soup.

▌Add the noodle to the kelp soup base with soy sauce, sugar, sesame oil and drain.

▌Start cooking the beef and mushrooms with a bit of oil. When beef is cooked, add carrot, onion and spinach, then stir-fry.

▌When vegetables are cooked, add the sliced egg. Mix the noodle with all the vegetables, and add sugar and soy sauce to your taste. Put it all in a dish and sprinkle some sesame seeds for the final touch.

Party Food

"Jap" means to mix and "chae" means vegetables. Japchae is one of the most favorite dishes in Korea for a gathering or a party. It originated from a royal dish. In the beginning, japchae was made with cucumber, radish, bean sprouts and bellflower roots. Today sweet vermicelli noodles are added to the mix. It is usually prepared with carrots, scallion, spinach, shiitake mushrooms, and green peppers. Beef may be added as an option but may be left out to be served as a vegetarian dish. The noodles are gray when raw and turn almost translucent when cooked (thus given its popular nickname, glass noodles). When cooked correctly, they retain a chewy texture.

Sweet Rice Punch (Sikhye)

Ingredients

12 oz barley malt, 2 cups rice, 7 oz sugar, *ginger, pine nuts, water

* marked ingredient is optional.

Recipe

▍Put the malt in a big bowl with water (4 liter) and scrub the malt with hands for about five minutes until the liquid mixture becomes murky.

▍Pour the liquid mixture through a sieve. Collect only the clear liquid below and discard the remaining malt in the sieve.

▍Cook rice. Pour the clear liquid that was collected above onto the fully cooked rice.

▍Let it ferment for about 5-6 hours (set the electric rice cooker to "keep warm"), until 3-5 grains of rice begin to float to the top.

▍Pour the rice and liquid into a big pot and add sugar and ginger to taste. Boil for 15-20 minutes. Let it cool.

▍Serve it cold and float a few pine nuts before serving.

Traditional Korean Beverage

Sikhye (also occasionally termed *dansul* or *gamju*) is one of the most cherished traditional Korean beverages. Sikhye is a traditional sweet Korean rice beverage, flavored with jujube and ginger, usually served as a dessert. In addition to its liquid ingredients, Sikhye also contains grains of cooked rice, and in some cases pine nuts. Sikhye was originally made from the rice that stuck to the sides of the cooker after the rest had been scooped out. It is a fermented drink made with barley malt and rice. Sikhye is made by pouring malt water onto cooked rice. The combination is then fermented for at least a day, and then boiled with ginger and jujube. It is served chilled. Sikhye is known to help the digestion of food and blood circulation.

Sweetened Rice with Nuts (Yaksik)

Ingredients

5 lbs glutinous rice, 14 oz dried daechu (dates or jujubes), 14 oz peeled chestnuts, 3 cups dark brown sugar, 1/3 cup soy sauce, 3/4 cup sesame oil, 1/2 cup pine nuts

Recipe

▎Soak the rice in cold water for 4 hours. Drain and steam for 30 minutes.

▎Cut the daechu and chestnuts in half.

▎Place the rice in a large bowl. Add the brown sugar, soy sauce, sesame oil, daechu and chestnuts. Mix with a wooden paddle until the rice is evenly coated.

▎Put the entire mixture back into the steamer and steam for another hour. Try one of the chestnuts to make sure they are cooked. If not, seam another 10 minutes or so before removing from the heat.

▎Put a layer of the sweet rice onto square or rectangular casseroles or other serving dishes. Sprinkle with pine nuts. Repeat making sure to sprinkle pine nuts on top. Let cool enough to slice into squares. Serve warm or at room temperature.

Appendix

Beauty of Korean
Traditional Costume

Hanbok

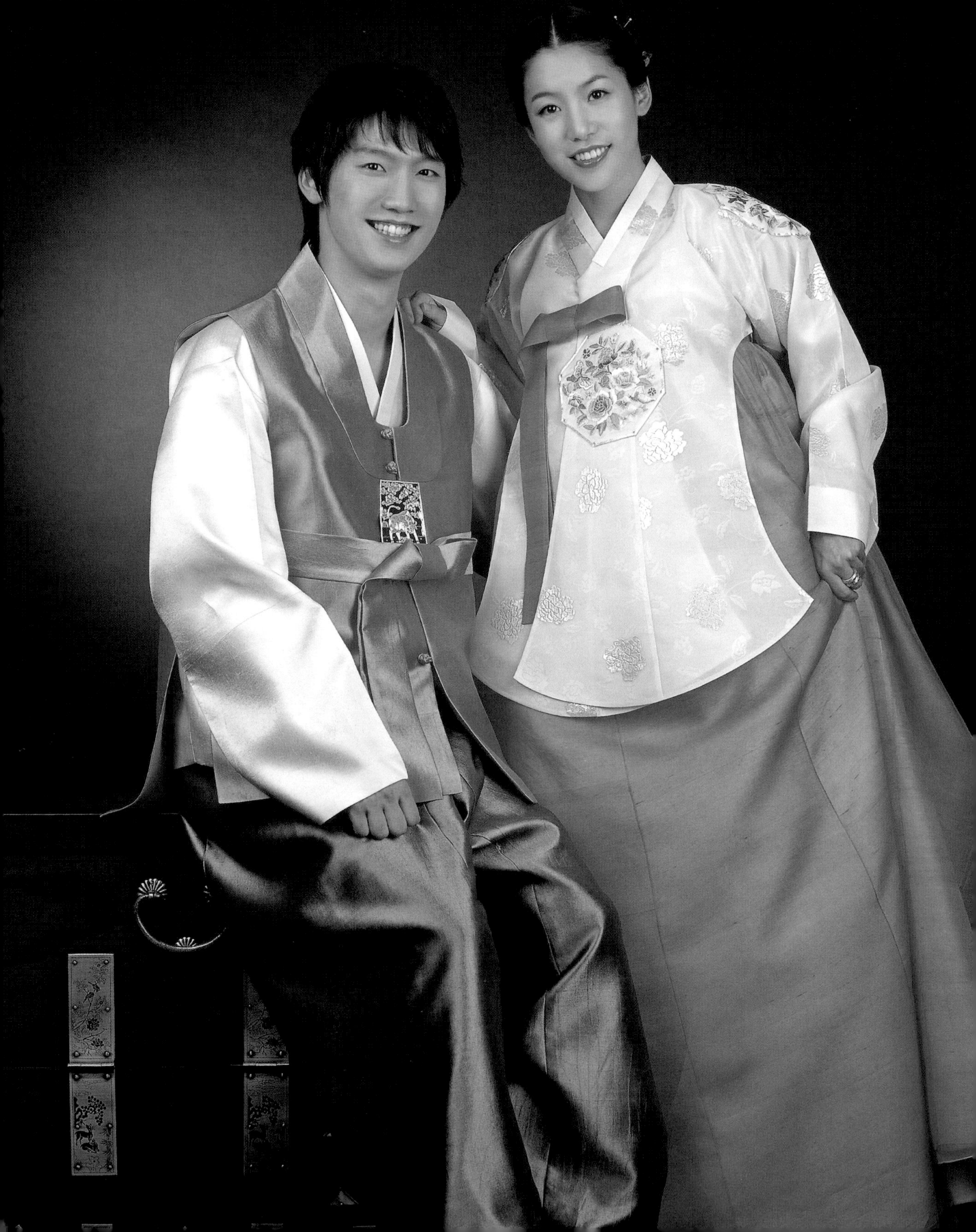

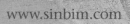

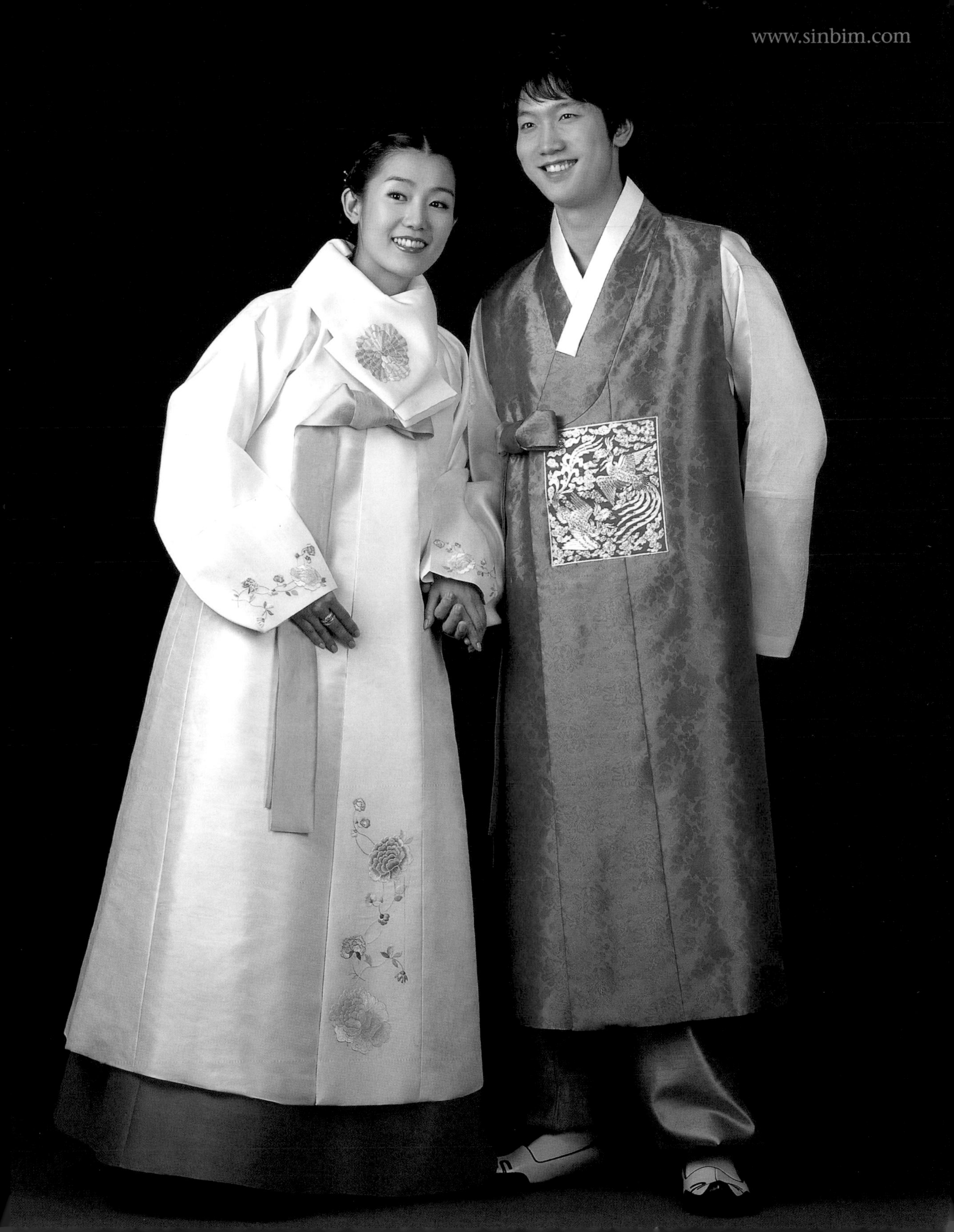

Korean Spirit and Culture Website

www.kscpp.net

All booklets published in the series are available on our web site, as well as additional materials covering various aspects of Korean history and culture.

Published so far:

Admiral Yi Sun-sin

King Sejong the Great

Chung Hyo Ye

Fifty Wonders of Korea

Online video library includes:

Korean Cuisine

Hanbok, the Clothes of Nature

Traditional Dance and Music

UNESCO World Heritage in Korea

KBS History Special Documentaries

And more...

Published by Korean Spirit & Culture Promotion Project

Korean Spirit & Culture Promotion Project is a 501(c)(3) not for profit organization that was formed under the Diamond Sutra Recitation Group (Chungwoo Buddhist Foundation) in October 2005 to promote Korean history and culture. KSCPP has been publishing and distributing free booklets and DVDs on Korean heritage. Please direct all inquries to kscpp@diamondsutra.org.

New York
158-16 46th Ave., Flushing, NY 11358
☎ 718-539-9108

New Jersey
190 Mountain Rd, Ringoes, NJ 08551
☎ 609-333-9422

Los Angeles
2197 Seaview Dr, Fullerton, CA 92833
☎ 562-644-8949

Atlanta
4619 Chattahoochee Crossing, Marietta, GA 30067
☎ 678-978-2331

Korea
131-80 Seongbuk 2 dong, Seongbuk-gu
Seoul 136-824
☎ 82-2-742-0172

Germany
Hiltistr, 7a 86916 Kaufering
☎ 49-8191-70618

England
57 Amberwood Rise, New Malden,
Surrey KT3 5JQ
☎ 44-208-942-1640

* When you finish this booklet, please donate it to a library or school so that it can be shared with others. It would also be greatly appreciated if you could leave your comments and impressions in the guestbook at www.kscpp.net or www.koreanhero.net. Thank you.